DACHAU CONCENTRATION CAMP

A Guide to the former Concentration Camp and the Memorial Site

Author: Nicolas Simon Mitchell

Front Cover Image
Liberated prisoners sing as they wait for bread
30 April 1945.

© Lee Miller Archives, England 2009.
All rights reserved.

Published by: Minerva Research, Sheffield,
United Kingdom

Designed by: Andrew Winter Design Limited
Printed by: Evolution Print Limited

ISBN: 978 – 0 – 9563202 – 0 – 9

Copyright © 2009 Nicolas Simon Mitchell

Nicolas Simon Mitchell hereby asserts and gives notice of his right to be identified, under sections 77 and 78 of the Copyright, Designs and Patents Act 1988, as the author of this work.

All rights reserved. No part of this work may be reproduced, stored in a retrieval system, or transmitted in any form or by any means, electronic, mechanical, photocopying, recording or otherwise, without the prior permission of the publishers.

CONTENTS

- 5 Introduction
- 6 The early years
- 7 The first prisoners
- 8 The SS and Theodor Eicke
- 12 The role and organisation of the concentration camp
- 14 Protective custody and admission
- 19 Who was imprisoned?
- 21 Work and the roll call
- 25 The barrack blocks
- 26 Medical experiments
- 28 The Memorials
- 35 The first crematorium and Baracke X
- 38 The Bunker
- 39 Liberation and the International Memorial
- 42 Conclusion
- 44 List of illustrations
- 45 Bibliography

DACHAU CONCENTRATION CAMP
Memorial Site

Arbeit Macht Frei ('work is liberty')

Introduction

This publication is designed to fulfil two functions. Firstly, to act as a guide to some of the important aspects of the history of the infamous concentration camp at Dachau, near Munich in Germany. Secondly, to highlight the significance of the main memorials that now stand on the grounds of the former concentration camp. These memorials provide silent testimony to the many thousands of victims who lost their lives there. These victims had the misfortune to cross paths with one of the cruellest, most vicious and murderous regimes that the world has seen. The ideology that under-pinned this brutal German regime was National Socialism (Nazism) and one of the key weapons in its armoury was the concentration camp.

Plate 1 The Museum Building

The early years

The first Nazi concentration camp opened on 22 March 1933, on the outskirts of the town of Dachau. Between 1890 and 1914 this small, picturesque, Bavarian town had been a thriving artists' community.

This situation was disrupted as many of its artistic residents responded to Germany's call to arms prior to the First World War; some enlisted, some moved away and the town never returned to its former glory. These demographic changes meant that the town felt an economic pinch in the period leading up to the First World War, and the town's patriarchs began to think of other ways to attract wealth and business to the area now that the artists and poets had left.

The answer to the void and its inherent impact on the local economy was the foundation of a gunpowder and munitions factory.[1] This new factory was known locally as the 'Pumf', and provided the German army with munitions for the battlefields of the First World War. However, defeat on the battlefield and the terms of the Treaty of Versailles meant that the 'Pumf' was closed down at the end of the war. The town of Dachau struggled in the 1920s; thousands of workers were laid off from the 'Pumf' or German Works as it was later called, meaning that the town suffered from unenviable unemployment figures compared with the rest of Germany. In later years the Great Depression compounded this problem.

By early 1933, the town's elders were becoming extremely concerned and increasingly vocal in their requests to the government of Bavaria to make some use of the site formerly occupied by the German Works. Initially, ideas such as a militia or conscription camp were floated for the site, but it was eventually earmarked as a concentration camp for political enemies of the newly installed Nazi regime.[2]

The origins of Dachau, the first Third Reich concentration camp, and the use of Schützhaft or protective custody, originated from an act of arson by a 24-year-old Dutch Communist, Marinus van der Lubbe.[3] The burning of the Reichstag in Berlin on 27 February 1933 presented Adolf Hitler, the newly installed Chancellor of National Socialist Germany, with a golden opportunity; it allowed him to present the arson as the signal that the Communists were

The first prisoners

preparing an armed mutiny against the state. In the wake of the Reichstag fire, measures were announced by Hitler and signed by President Paul von Hindenburg the following day. On 28 February 1933 these measures formed the decree 'Order of the Reich President for the Protection of the People and the State'. At a stroke of the ageing president's pen, the most significant law in the history of the Third Reich was implemented.

The huge implications of what Hitler had achieved with the Reichstag 'Fire Decree' were that this emergency measure abolished constitutional government. Germany was now governed under a permanent state of emergency, which was to last twelve years. It was a quasi-legal trick that underpinned the basis of the Nazi terror regime.[4]

The Reichstag Fire Decree was designed to protect the state from Communist violence. However, it also interfered in a catastrophic fashion with the Weimar Constitution, in that it suspended personal freedoms guaranteed under that system.

Penalties for acts of treason, arson and sabotage against the state now attracted the death penalty. Political opponents were now at the mercy of the Nazis,[5] and the first in the crosshairs of their gaze were the Communists, the Social Democrats, the Bavarian People's Party, royalists, journalists and lawyers of Jewish origin.[6]

These first prisoners were initially housed in local prisons, but this put pressure on the prison system because of the growing numbers of those incarcerated. The Nazis also feared that, if released, these prisoners would cause political unrest. A solution was found in the form of the concentration, or 'protective custody' camp with the first 'formal' camp set up at Dachau.[7] Prisoners who were imprisoned had not been tried and convicted; they were placed in the concentration camp as a preventative measure to eradicate subversive elements in Nazi Germany.[8]

Prior to opening the gates of the concentration camp on 22 March 1933,

---

[1] Harold Marcuse, Legacies of Dachau: The Uses and Abuses of a Concentration Camp, 1933-2001 (Cambridge: Cambridge University Press, 2001), p.18

[2] Harold Marcuse, Legacies of Dachau: The Uses and Abuses of a Concentration Camp, 1933-2001 (Cambridge: Cambridge University Press, 2001), pp.18 & 19

[3] Fritz Tobias, The Reichstag Fire (UK: Martin Secker & Warburg, 1964), p.2

[4] Joachim C. Fest, Hitler (USA: Harcourt Books, 1974), p.398

[5] Alan Bullock, Hitler: A Study in Tyranny (London: Penguin, 2005), p.263

[6] Helmut Krausnick and Martin Broszat, Anatomy of the SS State (St. Albans: Paladin Books, 1973), p.153

[7] Helmut Krausnick and Martin Broszat, Anatomy of the SS State (St. Albans: Paladin Books, 1973), p.149

[8] Helmut Krausnick and Martin Broszat, Anatomy of the SS State (St. Albans: Paladin Books, 1973), p.146

events had moved at a brisk pace in Bavaria. On 13 March 1933, a delegation of Munich Police under the command of Heinrich Himmler, at that time head of the Bavarian Political Police, inspected the former German Works in Dachau, and the architect engaged on the project approved the site as suitable for the future accommodation of protective custody prisoners. The site was cleared for an initial induction of 540 prisoners, and further room was then made to accommodate another 2,200.

The first police wagons arrived with 200 men who had been transported from nearby Stadelheim and Landsberg prisons. In the first fortnight, ordinary Bavarian policemen stood guard over the prisoners and the cruelties that were to become a familiar feature of Dachau Concentration Camp were not yet being practised – there were no beatings and humiliations in these first days of the camp. Prisoners were not allocated prison numbers as a way of identification, and work was not forced onto them. However, in April 1933, the Schützstaffel (SS) replaced the Bavarian policemen and by May of the same year, violence, terror and brutality had become the order of the day.

The SS and Theodor Eicke

The genesis and role of the SS is a hugely complex subject and any thing beyond a cursory explanation is way beyond the scope of this book.

The origins of the SS are to be found in Adolf Hitler's desire to have a group of men who would swear and act with absolute loyalty towards him. The first SS men were recruited in the early 1920s in each of the larger cities in Germany; by 1929 they numbered nearly 300. Four years later, in early 1933, when Hitler was intrigued into power as the Chancellor of Germany, the SS had quickly grown to 52,000 members. In those early years, the SS comprised what were regarded as 'the best physically, the most dependable and the most faithful in the Nazi movement'.[9] At this stage of the Nazi revolution in Germany, the SS could be best described as a better disciplined form of the Sturmabteilung (SA). These early SS men were fashioned into the armed SS, whom subsequently formed the SS Leibstandarte Adolf Hitler

[9] George H. Stein, Hitler's Elite Guard at War: 1939-45 (USA: Cornell University Press, 1984), p. xxvii

(Bodyguard Regiment), whose members swore a specific oath of allegiance to the Reich Chancellor. At the same time in other major German cities SS Political Purpose squads were formed, and it was from these squads that the core of the SS Totenkopfverbande (Death's Head) units emerged.[10] The first SS Death's Head unit under the command of Theodor Eicke was established at Dachau Concentration Camp in 1933. The SS Death's Head units were trained for concentration camp guard duty and the role, which Eicke played, is an essential element of understanding the organisation of Dachau and the wider concentration camp system.

Eicke's career rose on the basis of two key actions. The first, which brought him to the attention of his senior officers, was the effective manner in which he set about energetically organising Dachau Concentration Camp. The second was that he was prepared to drench his hands in blood, committing murder, as part of Hitler's purge of the SA in the 'night of the long knives' in June 1934.

The first action had huge significance, because Eicke's organisation of Dachau played a vital role, in that the rules that were devised and adopted in Dachau were to be later used as the benchmark for the treatment of prisoners confined in other concentration camps. Eicke effectively devised the model that was to be later implemented throughout the whole system of Nazi extermination and concentration camps.[11]

Many infamous SS concentration camp guards had been trained by Eicke, and he instilled in them a burning, passionate and intense hatred for the concentration camp prisoners

Many infamous SS concentration camp guards had been trained by Eicke, and he instilled in them a burning, passionate and intense hatred for the concentration camp prisoners; prisoners were, as far as the SS were concerned, 'the enemy behind the wire'.[12] Eicke's methods for treating the prisoners had not come out of a clear blue sky; he had taken up the rough and ready blueprint left by his predecessor at Dachau Concentration Camp – its first Commandant, SS-Oberführer Hilmar Wackerle. Wackerle outlined,

---

10 George H. Stein, Hitler's Elite Guard at War: 1939-45 (USA: Cornell University Press, 1984), pp.5 & 6

11 Charles W. Sydnor 'The History of the SS Totenkopfdivision and the Postwar Mythology of the Waffen SS', Central European History, 6 (4) (1973), 339-362 (p.342)

12 Charles W. Sydnor, Soldiers of Destruction: The SS Death's Head Division, 1933-1945 (USA: Princeton University Press, 1990), p.12

in written form, the draconian punishments that were to be meted out to the prisoners. Under Wackerle's early tutelage, the style of SS management of Dachau Concentration Camp was quickly established, and in just over two months after the first prisoners had arrived, there had already been twelve murders.[13] Wackerle was subsequently dismissed, after an investigation by the Munich Public Prosecutor's office into his role in aiding and abetting murder.

The murders that had occurred under his tenure caused political difficulties and adverse publicity. Wackerle was a liability to his senior officers, and he had to go.[14]

Eicke would not waste his legacy and he refashioned, refined and formalised the rules and regulations initiated by Wackerle. These were formally laid down on 1 October 1933 as regulations for the 'Maintenance of Discipline and Order'.[15] These regulations were to remain an integral part of the Nazi way of treating concentration camp prisoners until 1945.[16] Such prisoners were incarcerated and enmeshed in a system that meted out draconian punishments for infractions against rules and regulations which, although vast in scope, were often barely understood by the prisoners.

Through Eicke's devilish originality, many acts against concentration camp rules and regulations attracted the death penalty. For example, the death penalty was permitted for offences of political agitation, disseminating propaganda, escaping, attempting to escape, mutiny or sabotage and a whole gamut of less serious infractions. Eicke also implemented a series of other punishments including confinement in 'The Bunker' for periods of 8, 14, 21 and 42 days, bolstered by corporal punishment in the form of 25 lashes of a whip.[17]

The second action that played an enormous part in the ascendancy of Eicke's SS career was his murderous

---

13 Harold Marcuse, Legacies of Dachau: The Uses and Abuses of a Concentration Camp, 1933-2001 (Cambridge: Cambridge University Press, 2001), p. 22

14 Helmut Krausnick and Martin Broszat, Anatomy of the SS State (St. Albans: Paladin Books, 1973), p. 173 & 174

15 Charles W. Sydnor, Soldiers of Destruction: The SS Death's Head Division, 1933-1945 (USA: Princeton University Press, 1990), p. 12

16 Helmut Krausnick and Martin Broszat, Anatomy of the SS State (St. Albans: Paladin Books, 1973), p. 178

17 Charles W. Sydnor, Soldiers of Destruction: The SS Death's Head Division, 1933-1945 (USA: Princeton University Press, 1990), p. 13

role in the Machiavellian power struggles within the Nazi party itself, exhibited in the rivalry between the SS and the revolutionary militia, the SA. At one time the SA had vastly outnumbered the SS and tension existed between Adolf Hitler and Ernst Röhm, the leader of the SA, as to the direction of the Nazi revolution in Germany. Röhm wanted to take the revolution further, to inject the Nazi revolution with the socialism that its name suggested. Hitler backed away from Röhm's radical ideas, and recognised the political advantages of settling with the German army and other conservative elements in the country. Hitler knew the threat that Röhm and the SA presented and that Germany may well undergo a second revolution if Röhm continued to press for more extreme action. Hitler decided to act and he dealt ruthlessly with Röhm, his one-time comrade, and other key figures in the SA, in what has become known as the 'night of the long knives'.

In the manner expected of an SS man, Eicke exhibited his unswerving loyalty to Hitler by shooting Röhm in June 1934 in a cell at Munich's Stadelheim prison. Through these two actions, organising Dachau Concentration Camp and murdering Röhm, Eicke's career was firmly in the ascendancy. He was promoted to SS Gruppenführer, the equivalent rank to a Lieutenant General,[18] and became Inspector of Concentration Camps and Leader of SS Guard Units.[19] This meant that Eicke was able to export the rules for the treatment of concentration camp prisoners and organisation of the SS camp complex to other concentration camps in the Third Reich. The 'Dachau model' had been born.[20]

---

18 George H. Stein, Hitler's Elite Guard at War: 1939-45 (USA: Cornell University Press, 1984), pp. xxvi & xxviii

19 Charles W. Sydnor 'The History of the SS Totenkopfdivision and the Postwar Mythology of the Waffen SS', Central European History, 6 (4) (1973), 339-362 (p. 343)

20 Charles W. Sydnor, Soldiers of Destruction: The SS Death's Head Division, 1933-1945 (USA: Princeton University Press, 1990), p. 19

The role and organisation of the concentration camp

In the very early years of the Nazi regime, it was by no means set in stone that the concentration camp system would become a permanent feature of life in Nazi Germany. But by 1935, the political advantage and utility, which the concentration camp system gave to the Nazis, was crystal clear. It had been extremely effective in emasculating their enemies. Opposition from Communists, Social Democrats, journalists, royalists, trade unionists, Jewish lawyers and others had been ruthlessly dealt with in the first wave of arrests in the immediate aftermath of the Nazis coming to power. Some politicians such as the Reichsstatthalter for Bavaria, Ritter von Epp, argued for a reduction in the number of concentration camp prisoners, as they were burdensome on state finances. However, Hitler and Himmler recognised that the concentration camps were a potent political weapon. They had already been used with devastating effect to deal with rebels and dissenters to Nazism; additionally, they could be used for propaganda with reports carefully disseminated into the domestic and foreign press, in a form that would highlight the supposedly favourable conditions within the concentration camp. Articles were published stressing how hard physical work, combined with a robust lifestyle based loosely on military lines, could be used to rehabilitate citizens back into Nazi Germany.

Plate 2 Propaganda photograph from December 1933 portraying Dachau prisoners playing sport (courtesy of the Hoffman Archive, Bayerische Staatsbibliothek)

Plate 3 Propaganda photograph from June 1933 of prisoners building a swimming pool at Dachau Concentration Camp (courtesy of the Hoffman Archive, Bayerische Staatsbibliothek)

Despite the propaganda reports, the very mention of the name Dachau struck fear into many Germans. This short poem from 1935 highlights their attitude:

Lieber Herr Gott, mach mich stumm
Das ich nicht nach Dachau komm

[Dear God, make me dumb
That I may not to Dachau come.] [21]

As Hitler's foreign policy brinkmanship brought the prospect of war ever closer, the concentration camps were reorganised with Hitler giving the all clear for the camps to be financed out of the national, rather than state budget.[22] The impact of this decision was reflected at Dachau Concentration Camp in 1937 and 1938 when a process of demolition and rebuilding was undertaken.

The old stone barracks of the former German Works were demolished and replaced with 34 new barracks, built by the prisoners. The accommodation capacity at Dachau was effectively doubled so that it could now incarcerate thousands of additional prisoners.[23]

The rebuilding was completed on 15 August 1938. In the period between 1933 and 1942, before the huge influx of foreigners from all over Europe, prisoners had their own individual bunk space, a cupboard where they could store a few personal belongings, and the barrack blocks were equipped with stoves.[24]

Some privileged prisoners were also allowed to send two letters a month to friends or relatives in the outside world.[25]

Plate 4 Newspaper propaganda report regarding Dachau Concentration Camp November 1936 (courtesy of the Hoffman Archive, Bayerische Staatsbibliothek)

---

21 Morris Janowitz, 'German Reactions to Nazi Atrocities', The American Journal of Sociology, 52 (2), (1946), 141-146 (p. 141)

22 Harold Marcuse, Legacies of Dachau: The Uses and Abuses of a Concentration Camp, 1933-2001 (Cambridge: Cambridge University Press, 2001), p. 31

23 Harold Marcuse, Legacies of Dachau: The Uses and Abuses of a Concentration Camp, 1933-2001 (Cambridge: Cambridge University Press, 2001), pp. 32-34

24 James E. Young, The Texture of Memory: Holocaust Memorials and Meaning (USA: Yale University Press, 1993), p. 60

25 Zdzislaw Koziarkiewicz, Dachau Prisoner Correspondence (USA: R.A. Lepley, 1999), p.2

Rebuilding also meant that there was now a huge SS complex at Dachau, which included the caserns of the SS Regiment Upper Bavaria and the SS motorcycle battalion 'N' along with a training camp for the SS. After the outbreak of the war the SS complex at Dachau grew further and included a vast warehouse for the entire SS, a hospital, factories producing clothing and offices dealing with the pay and personnel administration for the SS Death's Head divisions.[25a]

The organisational model for the concentration camps in the Third Reich had been settled as far back as 1936, when the Inspectorate for Concentration Camps issued an order, defining the different sections of the camps and their responsibilities. They were divided into five sections; the Commandant's Office, the Political Section, the Protective Custody Camp (prisoner camp), the Administration Department and the Camp Doctor's Department.[26] Prisoners incarcerated in the protective custody camp occupied one section of the five comprising the concentration camp.

Protective custody and admission

By the time the Second World War had broken out, the SS had a large, well-established and efficiently organised compound at Dachau, of which the protective custody camp formed an integral part.

The secret police,[27] known as the Gestapo (Geheime Staatspolizei), were usually the organisation responsible for arresting prisoners, commencing a chain of events that would culminate in transport to Dachau and other concentration camps in Nazi Germany.

The Gestapo's favoured time for an arrest would be in the dead of night. A person would often be dragged from their bed, and then hauled off to the police station. Out of the huge numbers of people who passed through the concentration camps, very few had any firm idea what they had done to deserve such treatment. The prisoners' first period of detention was usually in the police station and this could last for a day, a week, or a number of months. Whilst detained, the prisoner would at some point be served with a pink piece of paper; this was the protective

---

25a Harold Marcuse, *Legacies of Dachau: The Uses and Abuses of a Concentration Camp, 1933-2001* (Cambridge: Cambridge University Press, 2001), p. 35

26 Helmut Krausnick and Martin Broszat, *Anatomy of the SS State* (St. Albans: Paladin Books, 1973), p. 183

27 George C. Browder, *Hitler's Enforcers: The Gestapo and the SS Security Service in the Nazi Revolution* (UK: Oxford University Press, 1997), p. 32

custody warrant, which stated the tenuous reason for their imprisonment, often couched in vague terms such as 'placed in protective custody for suspicion of treasonable activities'. After the protective custody warrant had been served, the prisoner would then have to spend still further time waiting in police cells or prison, again, days or weeks. Eventually, the prisoner would be taken to the concentration camp; sometimes delivered individually, occasionally with a handful of others, or as part of a cohort of hundreds and even thousands.[28]

Survivors testified that the period in police detention at the beginning of their ordeal, although a huge shock, was nothing compared with what was to follow upon their journey to, and incarceration within, the concentration camp system. A central element of admitting a prisoner into the concentration camp was 'initiation' and it usually took place in the period between leaving the local prison and arrival at the camp. Its purpose was a simple one; it was the method chosen by the SS of immediately breaking any resistance from the prisoners. They would be punched, beaten, whipped, slapped, struck, kicked, shot, gouged and pierced with bayonets, and from time to time prisoners would be killed. Bruno Bettelheim, a former Dachau prisoner and author of the acclaimed book dealing with the concentration camps, *The Informed Heart*, states that 'I never met a prisoner who had escaped this kind of initiation'.[29] The purpose of this brutal initiation to the concentration camp system was simple, and for those on the receiving end, terrifying. It was designed to crush any spark of opposition in the prisoners, to petrify and change their behaviour so that they responded, without question or hesitation to the orders and demands of the SS.

> **They would be punched, beaten, whipped, slapped, struck, kicked, shot, gouged and pierced with bayonets**

Prisoners arrived at the concentration camp in a number of ways; sometimes they were brought to the camp in a car, others arrived in uncovered trucks, some in police wagons, or for many, being marched through the streets of Dachau from the railway station. The SS Political Department was a filter through which the majority of prisoners were passed before entering into the

---

28 Eugen Kogon, The Theory and Practice of Hell: The German Concentration Camps and the System behind Them (USA: FSG Books, 2006), pp. 60 & 61

29 Bruno Bettelheim, The Informed Heart: Autonomy in a Mass Age (London: Thames and Hudson, 1961), p. 124

concentration camp system. This department was responsible for admission and the occasional release of prisoners and they worked closely with the Gestapo.[30]

The SS Political Department kept meticulous records regarding the

Plate 5 The Jourhaus (contemporary photograph)

vast majority of prisoners who arrived at Dachau Concentration Camp. This procedure lasted until the final days of the Nazi regime. Upon admission, each prisoner had their details recorded on a personal file, which included age, physical description, and any military or police record. Prisoners were fingerprinted, photographed and questioned to ascertain that they were telling the truth about the circumstances of their arrest and detention. In addition, the prisoner's Gestapo interrogation transcript was pinned to the file, along with other documents, such as birth, marriage and university degree certificates. Recording information in this fashion and in such detail, gave the SS a clear picture of whom they were dealing with. The main file relating to a prisoner was held in the safe of the SS Political Department, whilst the prisoner's file-card was kept where it could be easily accessed and the prisoner swiftly identified.[31] The prisoners were never allowed to see the contents of their personal file.

The SS Political Department played an unusual role in that both prisoners and other general SS staff regarded its officials with fear; they were the Gestapo's eyes and ears in the concentration camp. The SS Political Department was also to a degree separated from the main part of the camp administration, and therefore enjoyed a certain amount of autonomy. This meant that they could initiate their own regime of terror – they were required to give little, if any, explanation for their actions. Once a prisoner had been admitted to the concentration camp system, a later summons back to the SS Political Department could be tantamount to a death sentence.[32]

30 Eugen Kogon, The Theory and Practice of Hell: The German Concentration Camps and the System behind Them (USA: FSG Books, 2006), p. 53

31 Eugen Kogon, The Theory and Practice of Hell: The German Concentration Camps and the System behind Them (USA: FSG Books, 2006), p. 63

32 Danuta Czech et al., Auschwitz Nazi Death Camp (Poland: Auschwitz-Birkenau State Museum, 2004), p. 48

At Dachau Concentration Camp the SS Political Department occupied a long, squat building just outside the entrance to the Jourhaus (dayhouse). Once the admission formalities had been concluded, the prisoners passed through the central portal of the Jourhaus. This building therefore played a momentous role in the history of Dachau Concentration Camp.

The Jourhaus formed the physical barrier that marked two zones; to the west, the SS camp complex, and beyond this the outside world. To the east, the protective custody camp where the prisoners would be confined and subjected to a regime that inflicted upon them indefinite imprisonment, harassment, terror and torture.[33] In addition to the actual physical barrier that the Jourhaus presented to the prisoners, it was also the scene of brutal events in the daily life of the protective custody camp. It was a place where new arrivals were tormented, humiliated and beaten before being engulfed by the powerful Nazi machine. It was also the specific location where the daily tide of camp life could be witnessed. At the crack of dawn, in all weathers, the prisoners flowed through the Jourhaus gate as they marched off to work, and ebbed back many hours later to be counted and confined for another day. The prisoners returned in the evening exhausted and ravaged, often carrying dead comrades who had not survived the day's ordeals. As far as the prisoners were concerned, the Jourhaus was the central location of their tormentors' power.

Integral to being admitted into the protective custody camp was a visit to the Schubraun, the reception area. A Carmelite priest, Raphael Tijhuis, was arrested by the Gestapo in Mainz, Germany on Thursday 25 July 1940 and held in various prisons before being finally shipped to Dachau; this passage describes his arrival and processing on 13 March 1942.

'After some minutes we arrived at the camp itself. The heavy iron gates swing open and more screaming voices: aussteigen! It is March 13 and bitterly cold as rough wind skims the barracks and snow is cracking under our feet. Estranged, shy, and even a bit anxious, we have a quick look around, but there is not much time allowed. On we go again this time to the Schubraun, which means something like the reception office. In the Schubraun, other prisoners who are put to work there are waiting for us. The only thing the SS man does is walk around a bit, uttering a curse or some sarcastic remark, especially to the clergy who, like the rest, are ordered to undress and stand next to their heap of clothes until it is their turn. Of course, everybody must give his complete family register to begin with

33 Wolfgang Sofsky, The Order of Terror: The Concentration Camp (USA: Princeton University Press, 1997), pp. 60 & 61

and sign for whatever valuable he is carrying. The items are put in a big, numbered paper bag, together with shoes and clothing. We are told to remember that number, and all of us receive a note with a number on it. My number is 29388. Twenty-nine, three, eighty-eight. It might as well be a phone number.' [34]

Plate 6 The Schubraun (contemporary photograph)

Once through the Schubraun, prisoners were usually despatched to the shower room. At some stage closely linked with depositing their clothing and being processed into the shower room, the prisoners were shaved of all their bodily hair. There are conflicting accounts of this dehumanising process happening before and after being showered. It is sufficient to say that this brutal event was an integral part of the trauma of being processed into the protective custody camp. Prisoners such as Raphael Tijhuis also report that they were immersed in a vat of disinfectant fluid.[35]

34 Raphael Tijhuis, Nothing Can Stop God From Reaching Us: A Dachau Diary by a Survivor (Italy: Edizioni Carmelitane, 2007), pp. 73 & 74

An unnamed prisoner describes being showered:

'The douche was excellent, refreshing. The shock of ice-cold water alternating with scalding hot drove all the exhaustion out of my system for a moment. But then at a barked command, the business was over, it was the sense of freshness that

Plate 7 The Shower Room (contemporary photograph)

was driven out of my system. There was one towel for every dozen of us and as I stood waiting I began to shiver as I had never shivered before in my life. All around me there were others in a similar plight, only my trouble was far worse. They were at least able to stand. I could not. I had been badly wounded in the war and I was helpless without my orthopaedic boot. Of course the towel was soaking wet when it came to me, and, in any case, before I had a chance to use it there came another series of barks from the young SS men to line up, naked as we were.' [36]

35 Raphael Tijhuis, Nothing Can Stop God From Reaching Us: A Dachau Diary by a Survivor (Italy: Edizioni Carmelitane, 2007), p. 74

36 Unknown author, G. R. Kay, Editor, Dachau, (London: Wells, Gardner, Darton, 1942), p. 55

The issue of a prisoner's uniform was the next step in the procedure:

'... now we get a blue and white striped shirt, jacket, and a pair of trousers, socks (ah!), and "clogs," which have wooden soles with cloth or leather on top'.[37]

By this stage in the admission process, the prisoners had lost their liberty, dignity, property, clothing, bodily hair and their names. For the SS, prisoner numbers and later, identification patches were sufficient. They had also lost their independence and autonomy; the only thing the prisoners had not lost in the maelstrom was the freedom to die.

Prisoners were now faced with a labyrinth of SS rules and regulations; the consequence of transgression would be SS violence in the form of corporal punishment, solitary confinement or death. The rules were numerous, the punishments draconian. For the prisoners, the issue of a uniform and the allocation of a place in the newcomers' block, itself surrounded by barbed wire and separated from the rest of the camp, marked a milestone in their misery.

37 Jean Bernard, Priestblock 25487: A Memoir of Dachau (USA: Zaccheus Press, 2007), p. 12

Who was imprisoned?

Protective custody within a concentration camp was designed to strike fear into the citizens of Germany; it was the sword of Damocles hanging over the people, an exceptionally powerful weapon that was used to destroy any resistance, real or potential.[38] The first prisoners comprised three main groups; political enemies, a-socials and Jewish prisoners who were despatched to the concentration camp as part of arbitrary actions.

These early prisoners represented a cross section of German society and included Communists, active Social Democrats, Jehovah's Witnesses, clergymen, purged SA men, and citizens making derogatory remarks about the regime.[39]

The Nazi net widened and from January 1935 criminals had to serve 'preventative detention' on top of the time that they had already spent in a conventional prison. This measure was expanded in February 1937, when 2,000 criminals from across Germany were arrested, with many

38 Heinz Hohne, The Order of the Death's Head: The Story of Hitler's SS (London: Martin Secker and Warburg, 1969), p. 184

39 Raul Hilberg, The Destruction of the European Jews (USA: Holmes & Meier, 1985), p. 223

hundreds ending up in Dachau Concentration Camp. This cohort of prisoners was arrested on the orders of Himmler who decreed that a specific number of prisoners should be arrested quickly. The grounds and reasons for detention were left to the discretion of the Criminal Police.[40] The Nazis also rounded up 'a-socials',[41] the precise definition of which was never made clear, but essentially it comprised people who behaved in a manner not regarded as normal.

German society was now divided into national comrades and community aliens. These people were vagrants, beggars, alcoholics, the workshy, errant fathers evading child maintenance, pickpockets, juvenile delinquents, homosexuals, prostitutes, plus a whole host of other people who led a non-normative lifestyle – and gypsies.[42]

Gypsies faced double jeopardy. Firstly, because the Nazi racial laws of 1935 deemed gypsies to be an inferior race, and secondly, because they were defined as 'a-socials'. They began to appear in the camps in greater numbers from 1938 onwards under the measure 'Aso-Aktion',[43] which was designed to take 'community aliens' into the concentration camps.

Plate 8 The Wiener Graben Quarry (contemporary photograph)

Following this action in June 1939 a transport of 550 Sinti and Roma gypsies were taken into protective custody at Dachau Concentration Camp. Many of these prisoners were initially set to work in the Dachau plantation, one of the hardest work details in the camp, before being sent to Mauthausen Concentration Camp near Linz in Austria whilst Dachau was closed for a few months in preparation for the Second World War.[44] Many of this group of gypsies died in the notorious and deadly Wiener Graben (Viennese Grave) quarry at Mauthausen.

40 Helmut Krausnick and Martin Broszat, Anatomy of the SS State (St. Albans: Paladin Books, 1973), pp. 192 & 193

41 Eugen Kogon, The Theory and Practice of Hell: The German Concentration Camps and the System behind Them (USA: FSG Books, 2006), p. 30

In the late spring of 1938, Dachau was used to imprison Austrians and in autumn of the same year an additional 2,000 prisoners came from the Sudetenland.[45] However, it must be stressed that a constant feature within the prisoner population from March 1933 onwards were the Jews, who were categorised as such no matter the reason for their detention, and were marked out for the most horrendous and brutal treatment of any prisoner group.[46]

With the outbreak of the Second World War Dachau Concentration Camp was used to incarcerate an increasing number of prisoners.

In addition to the usual German political enemies there were now prisoners of war from Eastern Europe, France, the Balkans and the Soviet Union, as well as an influx of European Jews and gypsies. The main camp had grown to include around 100 other smaller sub-camps scattered across the southern part of Germany and Austria. At least 200,000 prisoners are estimated to have been at Dachau or one of its many sub-camps over its 12-year existence. The expansion in size of Dachau Concentration Camp and the growth of sub-camps is a reflection of the labour demands of the Nazi war machine.[47]

42 Nikolaus Wachsmann,' "Annihilation through Labour": The Killing of State Prisoners in the Third Reich' The Journal of Modern History, 71 (3), (1999), 624-659 (pp. 624 & 625)

43 Stanislav Zamecnik, That Was Dachau: 1933-1945 (Paris: Le Cherche Midi, 2004), p. 220

44 Barbara Distel et al., Catalogue for the Exhibition: The Dachau Concentration Camp (Munich, Germany: Comité de Internationale de Dachau, 2005), pp. 85 & 86

45 Barbara Distel et al., Catalogue for the Exhibition: The Dachau Concentration Camp (Munich, Germany: Comité de Internationale de Dachau, 2005), pp. 80 - 83

46 Barbara Distel et al., Catalogue for the Exhibition: The Dachau Concentration Camp (Munich, Germany: Comité de Internationale de Dachau, 2005), p. 83

47 United States Government Archives, Publication M1938, Concentration Camp Dachau Entry Register (Zugangsbuecher), 1933-1945 (2004)

Work and the roll call

Work was a constant theme in the concentration camps. Inscribed on the wrought iron gate that marked the entrance into the protective custody camp at Dachau were the words 'arbeit macht frei', translated as 'work is liberty'.[48] This cynical phrase was also inscribed on the gate at Auschwitz.

Some very fortunate prisoners did from time to time find themselves released from protective custody at Dachau Concentration Camp.

The reasons for their release were political rather than based on the intensity of their industry. Work was compulsory, and the only freedom which work gave in the concentration camp system was the freedom to

48 Wolfgang Sofsky, The Order of Terror: The Concentration Camp (USA: Princeton University Press, 1997), p. 61

Plate 9 Entrance to Auschwitz Concentration Camp Memorial Site (contemporary photograph)

die. Work ruined and exhausted prisoners, and as Wolfgang Sofsky points out, '... work was an instrument to shatter them, wear them down, break their power to resist. It was a means not of survival, but of absolute power and terror.'[49] Work therefore played a huge role in the Nazi concentration camp system and Dachau was no exception. All prisoners had to work, and the detail to which they were assigned had a crucial impact on whether a prisoner would survive or not. The outdoor work details were the hardest, and those that did not require any degree of skill, only demanding intense physical effort, were where the prisoners were at the greatest risk of being arbitrarily beaten. The Jewish prisoners were always given the toughest and dirtiest work details. When a prisoner entered protective custody, the prisoner's occupation was recorded and those who possessed a practical trade, such as bricklaying or carpentry, were in a slightly more favourable position.[50]

In the early years at Dachau, when it was predominantly used to imprison Germans, the only opportunity for labour was within the camp itself and

49 Wolfgang Sofsky, The Order of Terror: The Concentration Camp (USA: Princeton University Press, 1997), p. 167

50 Hermann Langbein, 'Work in the Concentration Camp System', in Dachau and the Nazi Terror 1933-1945, Vol I: Testimonies and Memoirs, ed. by Wolfgang Benz and Barbara Distel (Dachau, Germany: Verlag Dachauer Hefte, 2002), pp. 64-74 (pp. 64 & 65)

its associated workshops. If insufficient work was available, the prisoners were often forced to complete useless and demoralising work tasks, such as barrowing gravel into a large mound. Work made life in the camp insufferable because it exhausted the prisoners both physically and mentally; they had to work, effectively helping their enemies, on a meagre diet, for long hours with no pay. It turned the prisoners into pawns of their oppressors, placing them on the horns of a dilemma; if they tried to work harder to gain a better work detail and increase their chances of survival, they would be at risk of exhaustion or injury, which in itself could have the gravest consequences for a prisoner too ill to work as demanded by the Nazis.[51]

The roll call was another significant aspect of the torment faced by prisoners held in protective custody within Dachau Concentration Camp. It took place on the Appellplatz, the Roll Call Square. This was a place large enough to accommodate up to 40,000 to 50,000 prisoners at any one time; it was a huge expanse of ground where twice a day, morning and evening, the prison population was forced to assemble.

Preparations for the morning roll call began around 4 a.m., when the prisoners were roused from their beds in the barrack blocks by the sound of a klaxon.[52] They were then forced to frantically make their beds, go to the toilet, clean the barrack block, and the meagre rations, loosely defined as breakfast were distributed. The prisoners then had to parade on the Roll Call Square in rows of ten. The imprisoned priest, Jean Bernard, reports that as they marched out to the square the prisoners had to sing out one of the

Plate 10 Roll Call Square with a view towards the Jourhaus (contemporary photograph)

51 Bruno Bettelheim, The Informed Heart: Autonomy in a Mass Age (London: Thames and Hudson, 1961), p. 209

52 Jean Bernard, Priestblock 25487: A Memoir of Dachau (USA: Zaccheus Press, 2007), p. 35

camp songs.[53] No one was excused from roll call; even the dead had to be carried out on the square to be counted. Parading the dead was the SS's way of showing all the prisoners present that their lives were worth nothing at all, that they too could be dead by the end of the day. Thousands of men faced this torment daily, parading in all weathers waiting for the appearance of their masters, the SS, who had total command over their lives and destiny. The prisoners were counted and then pandemonium broke out once again as they rushed to their appointed places to form up into work commandos. Only when it was light would the work commandos march off to their respective locations,[54] passing through the Jourhaus gate to work in the plantation or the gravel pits.

The prisoners toiled until the late afternoon in winter, and early evening in summer, marching back to the camp for the evening roll call. The morning roll call was a torment but the evening roll call was even worse. The prisoners had, by then, completed a hard day's work, and now they had to stand at attention to be counted once again. If someone had escaped then the roll call went on for hours.[55] Death was a familiar visitor; as one prisoner recounts,

'... last winter there had been a roll call that began at seven in the evening and continued until four in the morning. In a driving sleet storm, the men had to stand rigidly at attention for nine hours. At least twenty-seven had died that night.'[56]

Plate 11 Reconstructed barrack block (contemporary photograph)

53 Jean Bernard, Priestblock 25487: A Memoir of Dachau (USA: Zaccheus Press, 2007), p. 37

54 Wolfgang Sofsky, The Order of Terror: The Concentration Camp (USA: Princeton University Press, 1997), pp. 74 & 75

55 Eugen Kogon, The Theory and Practice of Hell: The German Concentration Camps and the System behind Them (USA: FSG Books, 2006), pp. 75 & 76

56 Michael Selzer, Deliverance Day, The Last Hours at Dachau (UK: William Collins: 1978), pp. 132 & 133

Dachau Concentration Camp

The barrack blocks

Two grey-coloured reconstructions of the former barrack blocks now dominate the former Roll Call Square at Dachau Concentration Camp Memorial Site. These reconstructions are faithful to the dimensions of the 34 original barrack blocks, four of which were functional barracks and the remaining thirty used to accommodate prisoners. The prisoners built the new barrack blocks, completing them in the summer of 1938. They replaced the ten stone barrack blocks from the early days of the protective custody camp in the old German Works factory. The newly built barrack blocks had four sleeping rooms and were designed to accommodate 52 men in each room, with 208 men to a block. Each accommodation barrack had four day-rooms, two sets of toilets and two sets of washing rooms.

The rebuilding programme meant that the capacity of the protective custody camp grew from 2,700 to over 6,000.[57] In 1938, when the discipline in the camp in terms of management of the barrack blocks was at its most stringent, there was a maze of rules, which covered almost every aspect of life in the blocks from tidiness and cleanliness of the blocks themselves through to the prisoners' personal hygiene.[58] Breaching these rules would place the prisoners on a collision course with the draconian punishment regulations, which were in operation within the protective custody camp. From the first days after reconstruction, the barrack blocks were always occupied beyond their capacity. However, this situation significantly worsened from the start of the war. From 1942 onwards, with the influx of prisoners from all over Europe, the blocks were horrendously overcrowded causing disease, illness and death. Days before liberation, many of the barrack blocks held over one thousand men, with 1,800 sick men recorded as occupying block 30. On 26 April 1945, three days before liberation, there were approximately 30,000 prisoners held in the protective custody camp.

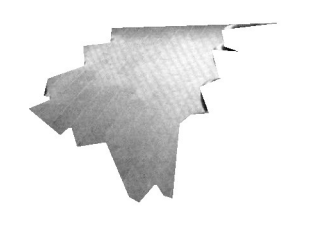

Plate 12 Reconstruction of washing facilities inside barrack block

57 Barbara Distel et al., Catalogue for the Exhibition: The Dachau Concentration Camp (Munich, Germany: Comité de Internationale de Dachau, 2005), p.103

58 Paul Berben, Dachau 1933-1945: The Official History (London: Norfolk Press, 1975), pp. 61 & 62

Medical experiments

Plate 14 Location of former barrack blocks

The location of the 34 barrack blocks meant that they were separated by the camp road, the even numbered barracks to the west and the odd numbered to the east.

The original barrack blocks were demolished over forty years ago; all that remains are individually numbered concrete rectangles, filled with gravel to remind survivors, relatives of the dead and others paying their respects where the barracks once stood.

The space between blocks 3 and 5 carries a particularly brutal legacy; this was where the Nazis positioned an airtight van, which was used to reproduce the pressure conditions to be found at high altitude. SS doctors carried out medical experiments on prisoners as a way to 'further the progress of German medical science'.[59] These experiments were conducted between March and August 1942, designed to test the atmospheric pressure a German air force pilot would face when rapidly descending from a high altitude, over 36,000 feet, without any oxygen.[60] Two hundred prisoners, mostly Russians, Poles, Jews and German political prisoners were selected for these criminal experiments, and 78 men were murdered as a result.[61] Other medical experiments, in the form of immersion-hypothermia, were carried out between the summer of 1942 and May 1943. These experiments involved freezing, and were conducted to examine how the human body could be re-warmed after being severely chilled. Iced water and dry freezing conditions were reproduced, and the effects of these conditions tested on the prisoners. In common with the high altitude experiments, these tests were linked to the progress of the war. The iced water experiments were conducted to assist the survival of German pilots and aircrew that were ditching into cold seas, whilst the dry freezing conditions were linked to the Soviet theatre and designed to assist German soldiers who were fighting in below-freezing

59 Paul Berben, Dachau 1933-1945: The Official History (London: Norfolk Press, 1975), p. 123

60 Vivien Spitz, Doctors from Hell (USA: Sentient, 2005), pp. 65 & 66

61 Vivien Spitz, Doctors from Hell (USA: Sentient, 2005), p. 66

conditions. These tests were carried out on 280 to 300 prisoners, and around 90 of them died.[62]

Gypsy prisoners who arrived from Buchenwald Concentration Camp in 1944 were forced to take part in equally hideous medical experiments involving sea water.[63] The sea water experiments were conducted on 44 gypsies from Poland, Czechoslovakia and Germany, whose ages ranged from 16 to 44; the tests were designed as part of an effort to make sea water drinkable through a process of desalinisation. The rationale behind these experiments was that if sea water could be made potable, then this could go towards saving the lives of German aircrew whom had baled out of their aircraft into the sea, and naval personnel clinging to the wreckage of sinking ships.

These experiments were conducted in the following way. 44 gypsies were divided into four groups; the first group did not receive any water, the second had to drink sea water, the third group consumed sea water which had undergone a technique called Berkatit (this merely concealed the taste of the salt but did not remove it), and the final group drank sea water which had been treated so that the salt had been removed.[64] These experiments were pure torture; prisoners suffered from a range of the most painful conditions including hallucination, foaming at the mouth, diarrhoea and in the majority of instances, madness and death.[65] The Dachau Concentration Camp malaria experiments were conducted over three years and involved 1,084 prisoners. The experiments were the longest running in the camp, commencing in February 1942 and ending in April 1945, and those forced to take part were from numerous nationalities, including a number of clergymen. Prisoners considered healthy (by camp standards) were deliberately infected with malaria either by blood, which was infected with the disease, or directly from mosquitoes. The motivation for conducting the malaria experiments was that it was one of the main diseases encountered by the Nazis in some of the countries they had occupied in Eastern Europe. These criminal malaria experiments led directly to the deaths of thirty prisoners. The ongoing side effects, difficulties and complications were later to cause the demise of three to four hundred prisoners who had been selected to take part.[66]

62 Vivien Spitz, Doctors from Hell (USA: Sentient, 2005), pp. 85 & 86

63 Stanislav Zamecnik, That Was Dachau: 1933-1945 (Paris: Le Cherche Midi, 2004), pp. 220 & 221

64 Vivien Spitz, Doctors from Hell (USA: Sentient, 2005), pp. 157 & 158

65 Vivien Spitz, Doctors from Hell (USA: Sentient, 2005), p. 173

66 Vivien Spitz, Doctors from Hell (USA: Sentient, 2005), pp. 103 - 106

Dachau Concentration Camp

The Memorials

Through the tenacity and dedication of the survivors there are now a number of memorials that dominate various locations on the site of the former Dachau Concentration Camp.

On the north-eastern side of the Memorial Site there is the unusual parabolic shape of the Jewish Memorial. It is appropriate to reflect on the fate of the Jews. The pace of persecution against the Jews in Germany began to quicken from the first days of the Nazi regime. They were banned from certain professions and the Nuremberg Laws of 1935 defined Jews in purely racial terms, blood being the determining factor. Religious conversion to Christianity, for example, would not exempt a person from being defined as Jewish under Nazi law. Prior to the 1938 Kristallnacht pogrom, German Jews were generally imprisoned in Dachau because of their political position and opposition to the Nazis. However, following Kristallnacht they began to appear in ever-increasing numbers in the camps. In the immediate aftermath of the Kristallnacht pogrom on 9 and 10 November 1938, 30,000 Jews were arrested throughout Germany and Austria, with 500 Jews from Munich[67] (16km from Dachau) amongst this number. These Jewish citizens were also taken into protective custody at Sachsenhausen (Berlin) and Buchenwald (Weimar) concentration camps.[68]

Kristallnacht marked the watershed for the treatment of the Jews in Germany. They were to play no further part in the economy of the country and were effectively banned from independent Jewish cultural life. The catastrophe of Kristallnacht for the German Jews was twofold; it firstly revealed that the Nazis had declared war on a section of the German people, and secondly that life for Jews in Germany, from then on, would become a futile struggle.[69] In effect, Kristallnacht was the spark that would lead to the flames of the Holocaust. Whilst in protective custody within Dachau Concentration Camp, the Jews were always given the worst treatment and the worst jobs. A prisoner called Gedye, who arrived in Dachau in February 1938, a few months before the Kristallnacht pogrom, describes the conditions and awful crimes that were already being committed:

'... in February, March and April there were a number of "suicides" and shootings "during attempted escape". The Jew Lowenberg was horribly beaten and

[67] Martin Gilbert, Kristallnacht: Prelude to Destruction (London: Harper Collins, 2006), p. 72

[68] Author not stated, Kristallnacht, Vol 10 Jes-Lei Encyclopedia Judaica (Jerusalem: Keter Publishing House, 1971), p. 1263

[69] John Mendelsohn, The Holocaust: Selected Documents in Eighteen Volumes: The Crystal Night Pogrom (USA: Garland, 1982), intro pages.

committed suicide that night. In March two men were shot "while attempting escape". The Jew Lowy was shot dead for approaching closer than the regulation six metres to a sentry who had called him up. Another was ordered by a sentry again and again to approach until he stepped on the forbidden neutral zone outside the barbed wire, whereupon he was shot dead'.[70]

These early deaths portended the treatment that the Jews would receive in Dachau. They would be dealt with harshly, callously, murderously and always on the receiving end of the worst treatment of any prisoner group. The final death toll for the Jews in Dachau itself is approximately 10,000. However, this terrible statistic does not tell the whole story because Dachau's Jewish prisoners were always being selected and sent to other locations where their fate was usually sealed.

The Jewish Memorial therefore stands as a testament and in memory of those Jewish prisoners who died at Dachau and other places associated with the Holocaust; it is positioned on the site of the former camp brothel. The sacral architect Zvi Guttman designed the memorial and it is constructed from black lavabasalt rock. It has an unusual shape and the central ramp is reminiscent of the death ramp at Auschwitz, the descent downwards into a dark chamber, evoking the image of the steps downwards to one of the dark subterranean gas chambers in Auschwitz.

Plate 16 The Jewish Memorial

The Jewish Memorial is designed to evoke the destruction of the Jews in architectural form. Over the entrance to the memorial are the words; 'put them in fear, O Lord: that the nations may know themselves to be but men. Se' lah'.[71] Black barbed fences skirt along each side of the

Plate 15 The Jewish Memorial

70 Martin Gilbert, The Holocaust: The Jewish Tragedy (London: Fontana, 1987), p. 58

71 Kathrin Hoffmann-Curtius and Susan Nurmi-Schomers, 'Memorials for the Dachau Concentration Camp', Oxford Art Journal, 21 (2) (1998), 21-44 (p. 40)

Plate 17 The Jewish Memorial

entrance and the same barbed effect can be seen on the main doorway.

The Star of David is visible on each of the gates, and brass olive branches act as handles, the olive branches symbolising God's reconciliation with Noah after the Great Flood. Once inside the dark chamber there is a single strip of light-coloured Peki'in marble, which leads the visitor's gaze upwards to the open sky and a menorah,[72] which signifies 'a sign of deliverance, the goal of eternal Jewish hope'.[73]

Dachau Concentration Camp Memorial Site contains a diversity of religious memorials; this is partly due to the large number of clergymen who were imprisoned and the effective lobbying of these survivors and others in the 1950s. The first clergymen who arrived in the early 1930s were generally only held for short periods of time – it was with the annexation of Austria that the numbers of imprisoned clergymen began to significantly increase.

Plate 18 Blessed Stefan Wincenty Frelichowski, a Polish priest who died in Dachau on 23 February 1945 (photograph taken by the author of an oil painting in Torun, Poland 2008)

The beginning of the Second World War also marked a sea change in the Nazis' attitude towards the clergy, and at the end of 1940 there were just over 1,000 clergy held in Dachau. At the conclusion of the war this number had increased to 2,720.

72 James E. Young, The Texture of Memory: Holocaust Memorials and Meaning (USA: Yale University Press, 1993), p. 67

73 Kathrin Hoffmann-Curtius and Susan Nurmi-Schomers, 'Memorials for the Dachau Concentration Camp', Oxford Art Journal, 21 (2) (1998), 21-44 (p. 40)

Polish priests made up the largest contingent of this number followed by the Germans (447).[74] The clergymen were generally held in blocks 26, 28 and 30 which were situated on the western side of the camp road. At the northernmost edge of the Memorial Site, under an archway topped by one of the seven former watchtowers, is the Carmelite Convent. This was dedicated on 28 April 1963 and consecrated on 22 November 1964. The confines of the convent courtyard and the peaceful church within provide a calming and welcoming respite for anyone undertaking a visit to the Memorial Site. Within the courtyard, displayed on the western wall, is the robe of the late Bishop Johannes Neuhausler, a former prisoner of the Nazis,[75] who spent four years imprisoned in Dachau.[76] Close to the Carmelite Convent is a large circular building made from rough stones from the River Isar. This is the Catholic Church 'The Mortal Agony of Christ', and the first religious memorial to be erected in the former concentration camp, designed by the architect J. Wiedemann. The church measures 12 metres high and has a diameter of 14 metres.[77] The church was consecrated on 5 August 1960 when over 50,000 people were present to witness the event. Prior to consecration 3,000 young men had carried the cross, which now sits above the altar, from Munich, in a replication of Christ's passion. Inscribed on the altar of the church are the words, 'to the honourable memory of the victims, for the atonement of the crimes, as a lesson for all visitors to the

Plate 19 Carmelite Convent

Plate 20 Catholic Church, 'The Mortal Agony of Christ'

---

74 Stanislav Zamecnik, That Was Dachau: 1933-1945 (Paris: Le Cherche Midi, 2004), pp. 166 & 167

75 Harold Marcuse, Legacies of Dachau: The Uses and Abuses of a Concentration Camp, 1933-2001 (Cambridge: Cambridge University Press, 2001), pp. 237-241

76 James E. Young, The Texture of Memory: Holocaust Memorials and Meaning (USA: Yale University Press, 1993), p. 64

77 James E. Young, The Texture of Memory: Holocaust Memorials and Meaning (USA: Yale University Press, 1993), p. 64

camp, for the peace of all nations'.[78]

On the northern perimeter of the former concentration camp is the architecturally impressive Protestant Church of Reconciliation, designed by Helmut Striffler and situated on the route to the former crematorium.

The church is now over 40 years old, having been consecrated on 30 April 1967. The architect designed the church to mark a stark contrast to the rectangular architecture favoured by the Nazis. It is also a place where visitors can pause for reflection and prayer as they pass through the Memorial Site.

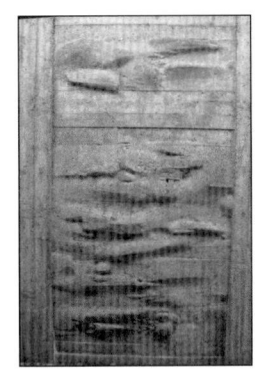

Plate 22 Bas-relief by Hubertus von Pilgrim

These reliefs are designed to evoke thoughts of the last journeys of the prisoners before their deaths. Twenty metres away in the passageway is sited a steel door, designed by the artist Fritz Kuhn and inscribed with the words, 'in the shadow of thy wings will I take my refuge' from Psalm 57:1.[79]

Plate 21 The Protestant Church of Reconciliation

Plate 23 Steel door designed by Fritz Kuhn

In a similar fashion to the Jewish Memorial, the architect has designed a descent into the memorial. In this instance, steps rather than a ramp bring the visitor to a pair of bas-reliefs by the artist Hubertus von Pilgrim.

Close to this steel door is a reading room and then the church itself. The inside of the church has an unusual architectural design; sloping floors and an exquisite stained glass

78 James E. Young, The Texture of Memory: Holocaust Memorials and Meaning (USA: Yale University Press, 1993), p. 64

79 Kathrin Hoffmann-Curtius and Susan Nurmi-Schomers, 'Memorials for the Dachau Concentration Camp', Oxford Art Journal, 21 (2) (1998), 21-44 (p. 39)

window by the artist Emil Kiess. The window is opaque glass with a solitary piece of red crystal, which is designed to suggest images of blood associated with birth and death. Also standing in the window of the church is a statue, called *Synagoga and Ecclesia* by the artist Franz Hammerle. The statue depicts a pair of figures, a mother and son, emerging from a single piece of wood.[80]

Above the altar in the Protestant Church of Reconciliation is an evocative, deformed cross, and the exit from the church is marked by an ascent past words in bronze embedded in the rough concrete. These words plead for redemption:

'Out of the depths have I cried unto thee, O Lord. Lord, hear my voice: let thine ears be attentive to the voice of my supplications. If thou, Lord, shouldest mark iniquities, O Lord, who shall stand? But there is forgiveness with thee, that thou mayest be feared. I wait for the Lord, my soul doth wait, and in his word I do hope' from Psalm 130, 1-5.[81]

The dome of the Russian Orthodox Chapel marks its location on the western side of the Memorial Site. The chapel was completed in 1995 and commemorates the Russian prisoners killed in Dachau Concentration Camp, and at the SS shooting range at Herbertshausen, approximately 2km from the main Memorial Site. The Russians executed at the shooting range were mostly commissars selected from amongst the ranks of Russian prisoners of war. These

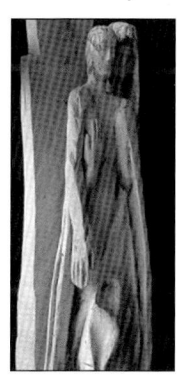

Plate 24 Stained glass window designed by Emil Kiess
Plate 25 Synagoga and Ecclesia by the artist Franz Hammerle

Plate 26 Deformed cross within the Protestant Church of Reconciliation

80 Heinrich Bauer et al., Protestant Church of Reconciliation: Concentration Camp Memorial Dachau (Dachau, Germany: Protestant Church of Reconciliation, Date of Publication not stated), pp. 24 & 25

81 Kathrin Hoffmann-Curtius and Susan Nurmi-Schomers, 'Memorials for the Dachau Concentration Camp', Oxford Art Journal, 21 (2) (1998), 21-44 (p. 39)

men were not officially recorded in the concentration camp records, and therefore the exact number of Russians murdered in this fashion is not known, although estimates suggest that it is over 4,000 prisoners.[82] The location of the Russian Orthodox Chapel in the area of the crematorium is also to act as a memorial to the

Plate 27 Shooting Range at Herbertshausen (contemporary photograph)

mass murder of 31 Russian officers on 22 February 1944, the murder of 90 Russian officers on 4 September 1944, and the murders of 2 other Russian officers a couple of days later.[83]

The following account contains the harrowing details of how the Russian officers were murdered on 4 September 1944 in the vicinity of the crematorium. The account is from the testimony of an SS man, Obersturmführer Friedrich Wilhelm Ruppert, made in October 1945, and which was used in the Dachau War Crimes Trials. Ruppert testifies regarding the murders:

'The interpreter ordered the first 15 prisoners to undress completely. He then told them to walk some 30 metres away from where they had left their shoes and clothes in a heap on the ground. There they had to kneel down in a line by a small heap of earth with their backs towards us. The SS who executed them went up to them and shot them in the back of the neck, each one executing several men. When the first 15 had been killed, prisoners working at the crematorium removed their bodies and took them inside the crematorium. The next 15 who had undressed at the same time as the first 15 were then executed in the same way. Then the guards returned to the gate and took the next group to the crematorium: the same procedure was followed for these 30 men and likewise for the last ones.[84]

Plate 28 Russian Orthodox Chapel

Near to the Russian Orthodox Chapel, in the grounds of the crematorium, is the first memorial erected

82 Barbara Distel et al., Catalogue for the Exhibition: The Dachau Concentration Camp (Munich, Germany: Comité de Internationale de Dachau, 2005), p. 156

83 Paul Berben, Dachau 1933-1945: The Official History (London: Norfolk Press, 1975), pp. 269 - 271

84 Paul Berben, Dachau 1933-1945: The Official History (London: Norfolk Press 1975), pp. 272 & 273

in the former concentration camp at Dachau. This is the sculpture of the *Unknown Concentration Camp Inmate*, the work of the German artist Fritz Koelle. The sculpture depicts an emaciated prisoner, with his hands thrust into his coat pockets, looking off into the distance. On the pedestal of the sculpture are words

Plate 29 Fritz Koelle's Unknown Concentration Camp Inmate

in German which translate as 'to honour the dead and to admonish the living'.[85] This memorial was placed opposite the crematorium building in April 1950 and finally dedicated in September of the same year.

85 Harold Marcuse, Legacies of Dachau: The Uses and Abuses of a Concentration Camp, 1933-2001 (Cambridge: Cambridge University Press, 2001), p. 194

The western side of the Memorial Site is the most sensitive area of all.

Close to the statue of the *Unknown Concentration Camp Inmate* is a small shed.

Plate 30 The first Dachau crematorium (contemporary photograph)

Contained within this shed is a double muffle oven supplied by the German engineering firm J.A. Topf and Sons of Erfurt.

This oven was originally designed for mobile use, but was walled in at Dachau, therefore becoming stationary. The design of the concentration camp ovens highlights the contempt with which the Nazis viewed the prisoners. Concentration camp ovens differed from conventional ovens used in normal funeral proceedings. They had smaller chambers, as coffins were not utilised, with the doors designed so that they could be opened manually and the bodies exposed directly to the flames. It was unimportant to the SS that destruction of the corpse caused smoke and smells. Fuel was often in scarce supply, and using as little fuel as possible was more important than black smoke and sparks emerging from the crematorium chimney as the corpses of inmates were destroyed.[86]

As the number of deaths in Dachau Concentration Camp increased, this small crematorium became overwhelmed. Plans were therefore implemented for the construction of a far more sophisticated building,

Plate 31 Double muffle oven inside the first Dachau crematorium (contemporary photograph)

which would be capable of processing living and dead prisoners.

The Nazis designed this building, which stands opposite the first small crematorium as Dachau's own murder factory, known as Baracke X. This building could accommodate the disinfection of prisoner clothing, the gassing of prisoners and a morgue where gold could be harvested from the mouths of the dead. The new building was also designed and built to house additional crematorium ovens.

The gas chamber at Dachau Concentration Camp was not used for mass murder, although the test gassing and the inherent murder of

Plate 32 Baracke X (contemporary photograph)

prisoners did occur.[87] The gas chamber was designed and built to hold around 150 prisoners. In the opinion of Stanislav Zamecnik, author of *That Was Dachau: 1933-1945*, the gas chamber was certainly used, ostensibly to test that it would work and in connection with the medical experiments of SS Doctor Sigmund Rascher. A former prisoner, Doctor Blaha, testified after the war that he was sent into the gas chamber at Dachau in 1944 on the instruction of Rascher and 'of the

86 Annegret Schule et al., The Engineers of the 'Final Solution' Topf & Sons – Builders of the Auschwitz Ovens (Weimar, Germany: Kessler, 2005), pp. 28 & 29

87 Harold Marcuse, Legacies of Dachau: The Uses and Abuses of a Concentration Camp, 1933-2001 (Cambridge: Cambridge University Press, 2001), pp. 45 & 46

eight people he found there, two were dead, three unconscious, and three had collapsed in a sitting position'.[88]

The use of the gas chamber at Dachau raises difficult and very sensitive issues, as Zamecnik writes in his book. This gas chamber was used to murder prisoners, but it was not used on a huge scale. This was because Dachau already had access to a gas chamber at Castle Hartheim near Linz in Austria, where prisoners selected as a result of the action Sonderbehandlung (Special Action) 14 f 13 were taken. This action was closely linked with and followed the

Plate 33 Ovens inside Baracke X (contemporary photograph)

T4 euthanasia programme that had already murdered 70,243 German people by the summer of 1941.[89] Doctors from the T4 programme were used within the concentration camps to weed out prisoners deemed undesirable. The first prisoners in the sights of the T4 doctors were 'a-socials'. However, new groups also became the subject of selections – these were the prisoners who were too weak to work, and other prisoners who were racially or politically despised by the Nazis and selected to be murdered. Selections were completed under the charade of a medical examination. Importantly, the prisoners were tricked into believing that the examination would lead to a period in a rest camp.

Plate 34 The gas chamber inside Baracke X (contemporary photograph)

In Dachau one such selection required that 'all camp inmates were marched in goose-step past doctors at roll call.'[90] Those prisoners who were selected as part of 14 f 13 were taken from protective custody within Dachau Concentration Camp to its own de facto gas chamber at Castle Hartheim where the murders of 2,674 prisoners were carried out.[91]

88 Stanislav Zamecnik, That Was Dachau: 1933 – 1945 (Paris: Le Cherche Midi, 2004), p. 289

89 Stanislav Zamecnik, That Was Dachau: 1933 – 1945 (Paris: Le Cherche Midi, 2004), p. 203

90 Wolfgang Sofsky, The Order of Terror: The Concentration Camp (USA: Princeton University Press, 1997), pp. 241-243

91 Barbara Distel et al., Catalogue for the Exhibition: The Dachau Concentration Camp (Munich, Germany: Comité de Internationale de Dachau, 2005), p. 134

The Bunker

Roll call, exhausting working conditions and selections were some of the horrendous events that the prisoners had to endure, and allied to these torments was the prospect of confinement in the Dachau Bunker.

The Bunker was a prison within a prison. It was designed to house up to 120 prisoners. The Bunker courtyard was one of the places where executions and corporal punishment in the form of 'pole hanging' was inflicted upon prisoners. Seven poles, with four hooks on each pole, were erected in the courtyard and prisoners were hung for between one and two hours, suspended only by their shoulder joints with their hands tied behind their backs and feet suspended off the ground. This procedure moved into the shower room in 1941, and then in 1943 the practice ceased,[92] because the Nazi regime needed all the available labour for the war effort.

The Bunker was a place where the SS inflicted unimaginable violence on the prisoners, a place where their violent, torturing excesses could be practised away from prying eyes.[93] Imprisonment in the Bunker was usually administered after corporal punishment. The most common period of detention was 42 days, with a meal every fourth day, although the length of detention and the food varied according to the caprice of the SS, some prisoners endured in the Bunker for months. The SS also indulged in a variety of tactics in order to prolong the torture of prisoners within the Bunker. They would fire guns down the corridor, beat prisoners, encourage guard dogs to bark so that prisoners could not sleep, and deliberately spill the prisoners' food as it was being distributed.[94]

Plate 35 The Bunker (contemporary photograph)

92 Paul Berben, Dachau 1933-1945: The Official History (London: Norfolk Press 1975), p. 116

93 Wolfgang Sofsky, The Order of Terror: The Concentration Camp (USA: Princeton University Press, 1997), pp. 228 & 229

94 Paul Berben, Dachau 1933-1945: The Official History (London: Norfolk Press 1975), p. 115

Liberation and the International Memorial

In the winter of 1944-45, the conditions in the protective custody camp at Dachau went from terrible to horrific.

The full military and political collapse of Nazi Germany was only a matter of a few months away. The incursion of the Allies into German territory meant that the Nazi regime was hastily evacuating other concentration camps to Dachau. These evacuations swelled the camp population, resulting in a huge influx of exhausted and near-dead prisoners. Typhus wreaked havoc in the camp, with 3,000 prisoners dead from the disease by early 1945.[95]

When the Nazi state figuratively crossed the Rubicon in the early months of 1945, determined to fight to the very last man, the fate of a huge number of prisoners held in awful conditions in Dachau hung in the balance. Allied aircraft were flying over the SS complex and the prisoner camp, whilst the SS were scurrying to cover up the documentary evidence of their crimes, with many SS preparing to make good their escape. Himmler wanted the prisoners killed, and rumours circulated in the camp as to how this would be carried out. Bombing, gassing and shooting were all possible. The prisoners' leaders were desperately trying to devise plans to cope with this dreadful scenario. It was clear that the Nazis could try and kill the prisoners or that they would force the prisoners to march from the camp to an unknown destination. The best hope for the prisoners was to remain in the camp and pray that the Allies would be able to liberate them before Himmler's plans were put into action. Many thousands of prisoners stayed in the camp, but for thousands of others, so close to liberation, a final and terrible ordeal was about to begin.

On 26 April 1945 at 10 p.m., after hours of confusion, a march of around 7,000 prisoners left the camp at Dachau.[96] The SS escorted this column of exhausted and bedraggled prisoners as it slowly moved southwards towards the Alps; those who could not keep up the pace were murdered with a bullet in the head. The prisoners on the death march, who were physically shattered, with many on the very brink of death, expended the last of their energies in a desperate struggle to stay alive. The United States Army eventually liberated this death march on 2 May 1945,[97] yet for many this came hours too late, and it is estimated that this

[95] Barbara Distel, '29 April 1945: The Liberation of the Concentration Camp at Dachau' in Dachau and the Nazi Terror 1933 – 1945, Vol II: Studies and Reports, ed. by Wolfgang Benz and Barbara Distel (Dachau, Germany: Verlag Dachauer Hefte, 2002), pp. 9 – 17 (pp. 10-11)

[96] Paul Berben, Dachau 1933-1945: The Official History (London: Norfolk Press 1975), pp. 179 - 187

death march claimed the lives of over 1,000 prisoners.

For those prisoners who remained in Dachau Concentration Camp, liberation came a few days earlier than their comrades on the death march. At 3.15 p.m. on the afternoon of Sunday 29 April 1945, the first US troops began to enter the camp. Some SS men were shot, and the prisoners celebrated their first taste of freedom with a show of flags, proudly depicting their home nations. To the cheers and tears of the prisoners, the liberation of thousands had been achieved.[98] Despite the joy of liberation, there still remained some hugely important challenges to be dealt with – ensuring that the overcrowded camp did not descend into anarchy, burying thousands of corpses and containing the typhus epidemic which was rampaging through the prisoner population. Despite the best medical efforts of the American liberators, a further 2,221 former prisoners died from typhus and other serious conditions in the weeks following their release from tyranny.[99]

The centrepiece of the Memorial Site, commissioned, designed and erected

Plate 36 Liberated prisoners, 'On the Edge of Freedom' (photograph courtesy of the Hulton Archive and Getty Images)

97 Stanislav Zamecnik, That Was Dachau: 1933 – 1945 (Paris: Le Cherche Midi, 2004), p. 367

98 Paul Berben, Dachau 1933-1945: The Official History (London: Norfolk Press 1975), pp. 193 - 194

99 Stanislav Zamecnik, That Was Dachau: 1933 – 1945 (Paris: Le Cherche Midi, 2004), p. 376

to remember all the victims who met their fate in Dachau is the non-denominational International Memorial, which dominates the area in front of the museum building. This work is called *In the Machine* by the Yugoslavian contemporary sculptor Nandor Glid, himself an orphan of

Plate 37 In the Machine by Nandor Glid

the Holocaust.[100] The commission to design the International Memorial was allocated by way of a competition, which was won by Glid. Inherent in the piece are three crucial motifs forming the brief that the competing artists had to work towards; suffering of the victims, solidarity, and optimism for the future. This sculpture, unveiled and dedicated on 9 September 1968, is 16 metres long and 6.3 metres high,[101] made of black bronze, with a mêlée of figures appearing as if caught in barbed wire, their mouths open in cries of anguish. Barbed wire formed an important motif in the camp, it physically enclosed the prisoners, yet

some prisoners ran into the barbed wire to commit suicide, the ultimate act of self-determination and resistance to Nazi terror.[102] Close to the barbed wire and human-looking shapes in black bronze there is a colourful sculpture that also forms part of Glid's work. The three large

Plate 38 In the Machine by Nandor Glid

links are designed to evoke images of solidarity in the concentration camp between the prisoners. The triangles symbolise the prisoner patches, which the SS designed and forced the prisoners to wear by way of identification. These prisoner patches were a crucial part of the humiliation that the prisoners suffered, in that their identity was reduced to a number and a coloured cloth patch on a striped uniform.

100 James E. Young, The Texture of Memory: Holocaust Memorials and Meaning (USA: Yale University Press, 1993), p. 66

101 Harold Marcuse, Legacies of Dachau: The Uses and Abuses of a Concentration Camp, 1933-2001 (Cambridge: Cambridge University Press, 2001), p. 259

102 Kathrin Hoffmann-Curtius and Susan Nurmi-Schomers, 'Memorials for the Dachau Concentration Camp', Oxford Art Journal, 21 (2) (1998), 21-44 (p. 43)

Conclusion

The latest estimate[103] of the number of deaths within the Dachau Concentration Camp stands at 41,566. This figure is comprised of 32,099 who are confirmed as dead by the International Tracing Service of the Red Cross, and an additional 9,467 persons whose deaths can be ascertained because of documents and other evidence such as mass graves where human remains have been found.[104] This figure accounts for at least 4,000 Soviet prisoners killed between 1941 and 1942, and 4,851 other Dachau inmates who were transported from the camp to be killed at Castle Hartheim and Auschwitz.[105] These figures do not tell the complete story, because researchers from the Memorial Site are currently working on a 'book of the dead', and are investigating the deaths of many as yet unnamed and unidentified persons who were forced onto the death marches in the final chaotic stages as the Nazi regime collapsed. It is anticipated that the number of prisoners who died in Dachau is higher than the existing figure, and it is very likely that the total number of deaths will never, ever be known.

---

103 Estimate by Stanislav Zamecnik within Barbara Distel et al., Catalogue for the Exhibition: The Dachau Concentration Camp (Munich, Germany: Comité de Internationale de Dachau, 2005), p. 206

104 Barbara Distel et al., Catalogue for the Exhibition: The Dachau Concentration Camp (Munich, Germany: Comité de Internationale de Dachau, 2005), p. 206

105 Barbara Distel et al., Catalogue for the Exhibition: The Dachau Concentration Camp (Munich, Germany: Comité de Internationale de Dachau, 2005), p. 206

Plate 39 Reconstructed watchtower

List of illustrations

Front cover Liberated prisoners sing as they wait for bread 30 April 1945. Photographed by Lee Miller

Arbeit Macht Frei ('work is liberty') (contemporary photograph: author) p. 4

Plate 1 The Museum Building (contemporary photograph: author) p. 5

Plate 2 Propaganda photograph from December 1933 portraying Dachau prisoners playing sport (courtesy of the Hoffman Archive Bayerische Staatsbibliothek) p. 12

Plate 3 Propaganda photograph from June 1933 of prisoners building a swimming pool at Dachau Concentration Camp (courtesy of the Hoffman Archive Bayerische Staatsbibliothek) p. 12

Plate 4 Newspaper propaganda report regarding Dachau Concentration Camp November 1936 (courtesy of the Hoffman Archive Bayerische Staatsbibliothek) p. 13

Plate 5 The Jourhaus (contemporary photograph: author) p. 16

Plate 6 The Schubraun (contemporary photograph: author) p. 18

Plate 7 The Shower Room (contemporary photograph: author) p. 18

Plate 8 The Wiener Graben Quarry (contemporary photograph: author) p. 20

Plate 9 Entrance to Auschwitz Concentration Camp Memorial Site (contemporary photograph: author) p. 22

Plate 10 Roll Call Square with a view towards the Jourhaus (contemporary photograph: author) p. 23

Plate 11 Reconstructed barrack block (contemporary photograph: author) p. 24

Plate 12 Reconstruction of washing facilities inside barrack block (contemporary photograph: author) p. 25

Plate 13 Reconstruction of toilet facilities inside barrack block (contemporary photograph: author) p. 25

Plate 14 Location of former barrack blocks (contemporary photograph: author) p. 26

Plate 15 The Jewish Memorial (contemporary photograph: author) p. 29

Plate 16 The Jewish Memorial (contemporary photograph: author) p. 29

Plate 17 The Jewish Memorial (contemporary photograph: author) p. 30

Plate 18 Blessed Stefan Wincenty Frelichowski, Polish priest who died in Dachau on 23 February 1945 (photograph taken by the author of an oil painting in Torun, Poland 2008) p. 30

Plate 19 Carmelite Convent (contemporary photograph: author) p. 31

Plate 20 Catholic Church 'The Mortal Agony of Christ' (contemporary photograph: author) p. 31

Plate 21 The Protestant Church of Reconciliation (contemporary photograph: author) p. 32

Plate 22 Bas-relief by Hubertus von Pilgrim (contemporary photograph: author) p. 32

Plate 23 Steel door designed by Fritz Kuhn (contemporary photograph: author) p. 32

Plate 24 Stained glass window designed by Emil Kiess (contemporary photograph: author) p. 33

Plate 25 Synagoga and Ecclesia by the artist Franz Hammerle (contemporary photograph: author) p. 33

Plate 26 Deformed cross within the Protestant Church of Reconciliation (contemporary photograph: author) p. 33

List of illustrations - continued

Plate 27 Shooting range at Herbertshausen (contemporary photograph: author) p. 34

Plate 28 Russian Orthodox Chapel (contemporary photograph: author) p. 34

Plate 29 Fritz Koelle's Unknown Concentration Camp Inmate (contemporary photograph: author) p. 35

Plate 30 The first Dachau crematorium (contemporary photograph: author) p. 35

Plate 31 Double muffle oven inside the first Dachau crematorium (contemporary photograph: author) p. 36

Plate 32 Baracke X (contemporary photograph: author) p. 36

Plate 33 Ovens inside Baracke X (contemporary photograph: author) p. 37

Plate 34 The gas chamber inside Baracke X (contemporary photograph: author) p. 37

Plate 35 The Bunker (contemporary photograph: author) p. 38

Plate 36 Liberated prisoners 'On the Edge of Freedom' (photograph courtesy of the Hulton Archive and Getty Images) p. 40

Plate 37 In the Machine by Nandor Glid (contemporary photograph: author) p. 41

Plate 38 In the Machine by Nandor Glid (contemporary photograph: author) p. 41

Plate 39 Reconstructed watchtower (contemporary photograph: author) p. 43

Back cover Never Again – Dachau Concentration Camp Memorial Site (contemporary photograph: author)

Bibliography

Bauer, Heinrich et al. Date of publication not stated. Protestant Church of Reconciliation: Concentration Camp Memorial Dachau (Dachau, Germany: Protestant Church of Reconciliation)

Benz, Wolfgang., and Barbara Distel (eds.). 2002. Dachau and the Nazi Terror 1933 – 1945, Vol I: Testimonies and Memoirs (Dachau, Germany: Verlag Dachauer Hefte)

───── 2002. Dachau and the Nazi Terror 1933 – 1945, Vol II: Studies and Reports (Dachau, Germany: Verlag Dachauer Hefte)

Berben, Paul. 1975. Dachau 1933-1945: The Official History (London: Norfolk Press)

Bernard, Jean. 2007. Priestblock 25487: A Memoir of Dachau (USA: Zaccheus Press)

Bettelheim, Bruno. 1961. The Informed Heart: Autonomy in a Mass Age (London: Thames and Hudson)

Bullock, Alan. 2005. Hitler: A Study in Tyranny (London: Penguin)

Browder, George C. 1997. Hitler's Enforcers: The Gestapo and the SS Security Service in the Nazi Revolution (UK: Oxford University Press)

Czech, Danuta et al. 2004. Auschwitz Nazi Death Camp (Poland: Auschwitz-Birkenau State Museum)

Distel, Barbara (ed.) et al. 2005. Catalogue for the Exhibition: The Dachau Concentration Camp (Munich, Germany: Comité International de Dachau)

Fest, Joachim C. 1974. Hitler (USA: Harcourt Books)

Gilbert, Martin. 1987. The Holocaust: The Jewish Tragedy (London: Fontana)

Gilbert, Martin. 2006. Kristallnacht: Prelude to Destruction (London: Harper Collins)

Hilberg, Raul. 1985. The Destruction of the European Jews (USA: Holmes & Meier)

Bibliography - continued

Hoffmann-Curtius, Kathrin, and Susan Nurmi-Schomers. 1998. 'Memorials for the Dachau Concentration Camp', Oxford Art Journal, 21(2): 21-44

Hohne, Heinz. 1969. The Order of the Death's Head: The Story of Hitler's SS (London: Martin Secker & Warburg)

Janowitz, Morris. 1946. 'German Reactions to Nazi Atrocities', The American Journal of Sociology, 52 (2): 141-146

Jes-Lei Encyclopedia Judaica. 1971. (Jerusalem: Keter Publishing House)

Kay, G. R. (ed.). 1942. Dachau (London: Wells, Gardner, Darton)

Kogon, Eugen. 2006. The Theory and Practice of Hell: The German Concentration Camps and the System behind Them (USA: FSG Books)

Koziarkiewicz, Zdzislaw. 1999. Dachau Prisoner Correspondence (USA: R.A. Lepley)

Krausnick, Helmut, and Martin Broszat. 1973. Anatomy of the SS State (St. Albans: Paladin Books)

MacLean, French L. 1999. The Camp Men: The SS Officers Who Ran the Nazi Concentration Camp System (USA: Schiffer Military History)

Marcuse, Harold. 2001. Legacies of Dachau: The Uses and Abuses of a Concentration Camp, 1933-2001 (Cambridge: Cambridge University Press)

Mendelsohn, John. 1982. The Holocaust: Selected Documents in Eighteen Volumes: The Crystal Night Pogrom (USA: Garland)

Noakes, J. and Pridham, G. (eds.). 2000. Nazism 1919-1945: Volume 2: State, Economy and Society 1933-1939: A Documentary Reader (UK: University of Exeter)

Schule, Annegret et al. 2005. The Engineers of the 'Final Solution' Topf & Sons – Builders of the Auschwitz Ovens (Weimar, Germany: Kessler)

Selzer, Michael. 1978. Deliverance Day, The Last Hours at Dachau (UK: William Collins)

Sofsky, Wolfgang. 1997. The Order of Terror: The Concentration Camp (USA: Princeton University Press)

Spitz, Vivien. 2005. Doctors from Hell (USA: Sentient)

Stein, George H. 1984. Hitler's Elite Guard at War: 1939-1945 (USA: Cornell University Press)

Sydnor, Charles W. 1973. 'The History of the SS Totenkopfdivision and the Postwar Mythology of the Waffen SS', Central European History, 6 (4): 339-362

Sydnor, Charles W. 1990. Soldiers of Destruction: The SS Death's Head Division, 1933-1945 (USA: Princeton University Press)

Tijhuis, Raphael. 2007. Nothing Can Stop God From Reaching Us: A Dachau Diary by a Survivor (Italy: Edizioni Carmelitane)

Tobias, Fritz. 1964. The Reichstag Fire (UK: Martin Secker & Warburg)

United States Government Archives, Publication M1938. 2004. Concentration Camp Dachau Entry Register (Zugangsbuecher) 1933-1945

Wachsmann, Nikolaus. 1999. ' "Annihilation through Labour": The Killing of State Prisoners in the Third Reich' The Journal of Modern History, 71 (3): 624-659

Young, James E. 1993. The Texture of Memory: Holocaust Memorials and Meaning (USA: Yale University Press)

Zamecnik, Stanislav. 2004. That Was Dachau: 1933 – 1945 (Paris: Le Cherche Midi)

Dachau Concentration Camp

Notes

Notes